JUL - - 2007

D1163125

Roll, Slope, and Slide

A Book About Ramps

by Michael Dahl   illustrated by Denise Shea

Special thanks to our advisers for their expertise:

Youwen Xu, Professor
Department of Physics and Astronomy
Minnesota State University, Mankato, Minn.

Susan Kesselring, M.A.
Literacy Educator
Rosemount–Apple Valley–Eagan (Minnesota) School District

PICTURE WINDOW BOOKS
Minneapolis, Minnesota

Editor: Jacqueline Wolfe
Designer: Joseph Anderson
Creative Director: Keith Griffin
Editorial Director: Carol Jones
The illustrations in this book were created digitally.

Picture Window Books
5115 Excelsior Boulevard
Suite 232
Minneapolis, MN 55416
877-845-8392
www.picturewindowbooks.com

Printed in the United States of America.

Library of Congress Cataloging-in-Publication Data
Dahl, Michael.
Roll, slope, and slide : a book about ramps / by Michael Dahl ; illustrated by Denise Shea.
p. cm. — (Amazing science)
Includes bibliographical references and index.
ISBN 1-4048-1304-7 (hard cover)
1. Inclined planes—Juvenile literature. I. Shea, Denise. II. Title. III. Series.
TJ147.D325 2005
621.8'11—dc22   2005024974

Table of Contents

New neighbors are moving into the house across the street. Heavy furniture is carried down long, metal ramps.

In the park, the new kids are gliding down a steep, smooth slide.

Everyone is using ramps.

What Is a Ramp?

A ramp is one type of inclined plane. An inclined plane is a simple machine with a flat surface that always has one end higher than the other end. Simple machines help people do work.

Ramps help people move heavy things from a higher place to a lower place, or from a lower place to a higher place. Ramps can be fun to ride, too!

Ramps

Smooth, straight ramps help animals climb into and out of trucks and trailers.

Long, moving ramps guide luggage onto waiting airplanes.

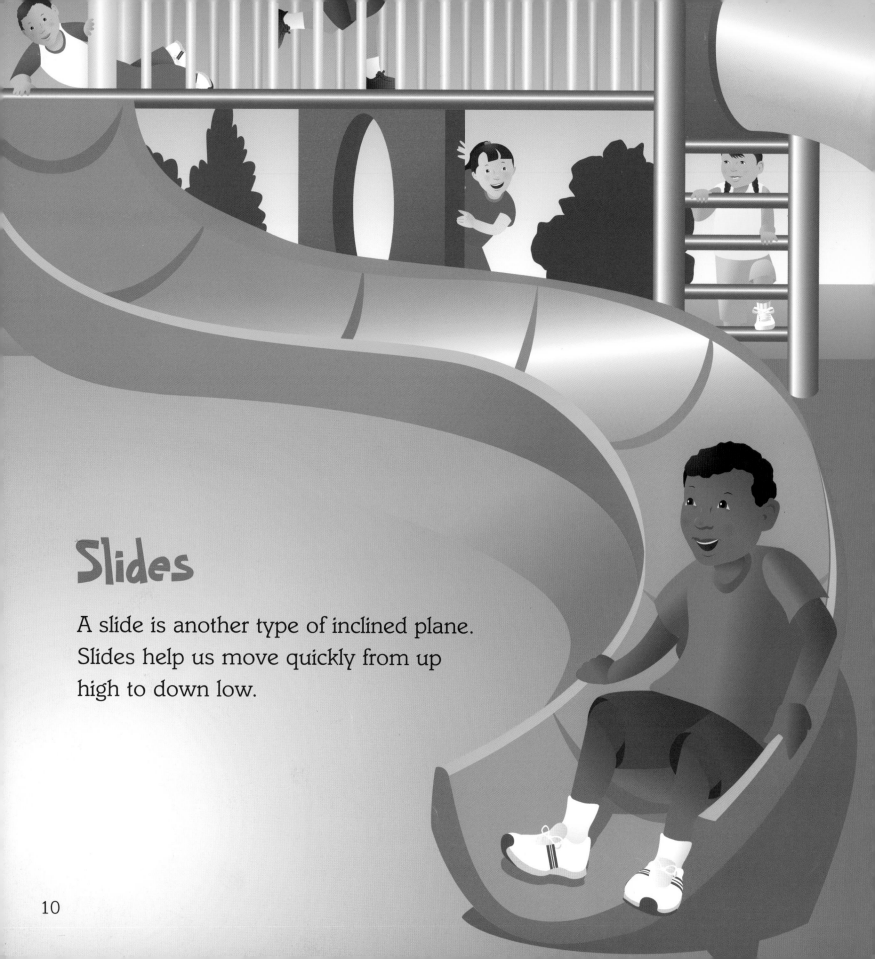

Slides

A slide is another type of inclined plane.
Slides help us move quickly from up
high to down low.

Some businesses use slides to move packages from one floor of a building to another floor.

Access Ramps

Ramps can also help move people and goods. People using wheelchairs, pushing strollers, or moving delivery carts can use ramps to enter and exit buildings.

Steep and Gentle Slopes

Inclined planes slope up from one end to the other. If an inclined plane has a gentle slope, things are easier to move upward.

If an inclined plane has a steep slope, things are harder to move up the plane.

Moving Traffic Up and Down

A highway becomes an inclined plane when it travels up steep hills or down gentle valleys. The inclined plane of the road helps traffic move smoothly from a lower point to a higher point.

Entrance and exit ramps are another kind of inclined plane. Cars and trucks move up or down a ramp to join the swiftly moving traffic on a highway or freeway.

16

Slippery Slopes

Inclined planes help protect houses. If the slanting roof did not help rainwater run off, the water would build up. Pooled, or built up, water could damage a roof and cause leaking.

Kitchen sinks, bathtubs, and swimming pools all have bottoms that are inclined planes. The gentle slope leads the water toward the drain.

19

Roller Coasters

Watch the roller coaster cars climb higher and higher. A ramp leads them gently upward toward the sky.

20

Then slowly, another inclined plane begins to guide them back down. Gently at first, then swoosh!

21

How Ramps Help

MATERIALS:

spring scale
weight
ruler (1ft)
shoebox
yardstick

1. Place the shoebox on a table.
2. Place one end of the ruler on top of the shoebox and the other end
   of the ruler on the table.
3. Put the weight on the lower end of the ruler.
4. Attach the spring scale to the weight.
5. Slowly move the weight up the inclined plane to rest on the top of the shoebox.
6. Read the spring scale as you move the weight.
7. Next, replace the foot ruler with the yardstick.
8. Repeat steps 3-6.

FOLLOW UP QUESTIONS:

1. What did you observe?
2. Why do you think that happened?
3. What do you think would happen if you used something
   shorter than a ruler or longer than a yard stick?

Fun Facts

- A plane is any flat surface, like a wooden plank, floor, or tabletop. Inclined means something that slants.

- Gravity is the force that pulls everything down toward the ground. Ramps make it easier to push or move against gravity.

- The slope of a road is sometimes called the grade. A steep grade makes the engine work harder as the car or truck climbs the ramp.

Glossary

goods—something useful

grade—the slope of the road

gravity—the force that pulls objects toward the earth's surface

inclined plane—a simple machine with a flat surface that always has one end higher than the other end

ramp—a type of inclined plane that helps do work; a flat surface that always has one end higher than another

slope—an upward or downward degree of slant

23

To Learn More

AT THE LIBRARY

Douglas, Lloyd G. *What Is a Plane?* New York:
  Children's Press, 2002.

Mason, Adrienne & Deborah Hodge. *Simple Machines.*
  New York: Kids Can Press, 2000.

Oxlade, Chris. *Ramps and Wedges.* Chicago, Ill.
  Heinemann, 2003.

ON THE WEB

FactHound offers a safe, fun way to find Internet sites
related to this book. All of the sites on FactHound
have been researched by our staff.

1. Visit *www.facthound.com*
2. Type in this special code for age-appropriate
   sites: *1404813047*
3. Click on the FETCH IT button. Your trusty
   FactHound will fetch the best sites for you!

LOOK FOR ALL OF THE BOOKS IN THE AMAZING SCIENCE SERIES:

Air: Outside, Inside, and All Around	1-4048-0248-7	Pull, Lift, and Lower: A Book about Pulleys	1-4048-1305-5
Cut, Chop, and Stop: A Book About Wedges	1-4048-1307-1	Rocks: Hard, Soft, Smooth, and Rough	1-4048-0015-8
Dirt: The Scoop on Soil	1-4048-0012-3	Roll, Slope, and Slide: A Book About Ramps	1-4048-1304-7
Electricity: Bulbs, Batteries, and Sparks	1-4048-0245-2	Scoop, Seesaw, and Raise: A Book About Levers	1-4048-1303-9
Energy: Heat, Light, and Fuel	1-4048-0249-5	Sound: Loud, Soft, High, and Low	1-4048-0016-6
Light: Shadows, Mirrors, and Rainbows	1-4048-0013-1	Temperature: Heating Up and Cooling Down	1-4048-0247-9
Magnets: Pulling Together, Pushing Apart	1-4048-0014-X	Tires, Spokes, and Sprockets: A Book About Wheels	1-4048-1308-X
Matter: See It, Touch It, Taste It, Smell It	1-4048-0246-0	Twist, Dig, and Drill: A Book About Screws	1-4048-1306-3
Motion: Push and Pull, Fast and Slow	1-4048-0250-9	Water: Up, Down, and All Around	14048-0017-4a